*To Adel,
Thank you
for your excellent
care.*

That's a Good Question!

Succinct Answers to Spiritual Questions

D1269506

PUBLISHING

Belleville, Ontario, Canada

That's a Good Question!

Copyright © 2005, Rick Reed

First printing May 2005
Second printing November 2005

Originally published as a series of articles in the *Ottawa Citizen*.

Library and Archives Canada Cataloguing in Publication

Reed, Rick, 1957-
That's a good question : succinct answers to spiritual questions / Rick Reed.

Originally published as a series of columns in the Ottawa Citizen.
Includes bibliographical references.
ISBN 1-55306-968-4

1. Christianity--Essence, genius, nature. I. Title.

BR96.R43 2005   230   C2005-902740-1

For more information or to order additional copies, please contact:

Metropolitan Bible Church
453 Bank St.
Ottawa, ON K2P 1Y9
613 238 8182

Essence Publishing is a Christian Book Publisher dedicated to furthering the work of Christ through the written word. For more information, contact:
20 Hanna Court, Belleville, Ontario, Canada K8P 5J2.
Phone: 1-800-238-6376. Fax: (613) 962-3055.
E-mail: publishing@essencegroup.com
Internet: www.essencegroup.com

To my dad and mom—

Thank you for introducing me
to the One who is the Answer
to life's ultimate questions

Introduction

How should we pray?

What's the difference between superstition and faith?

Do all sins have equal weight?

When is anger righteous and acceptable?

Is there such as thing as ultimate truth?

These are just a few of the good questions you'll find in this book. Each question was submitted by a reader of the *Ottawa Citizen*. For several years, the newspaper has run a Saturday column entitled, "Ask the Religion Experts."

While I'm uncomfortable with the title "expert," I've been happy to be a contributor to this column. It's been challenging to give a compact answer to a complex question (we're limited to several hundred words). I realize my answers aren't exhaustive; but neither will they be exhausting! My goal is to direct you down a trail that leads to Truth.

It's an honour to interact with people who have honest questions. I hope you'll find some of your questions asked in the following pages. And I pray that you'll discover answers that will make a lasting, spiritual difference in your life.

Rick Reed
January 2005

Why do human beings need religion?

To say that humans need religion is a bit like saying a thirsty man needs a cup. His real need is not for the cup but for what's in it. The cup is just the container for what he needs most: life-giving water.

As humans we have a chronic spiritual thirst. This thirst can only be quenched by God. He is the living water our souls crave.

Religion claims to be the cup where parched men and women can find the God they thirst for. Sadly, religion has often proven to be a cracked, dusty or even empty container. Many religious people have found that rules and rituals can't satisfy their thirst for God. They resonate with Bono's words: "I still haven't found what I'm looking for."

Jesus was speaking to religious people when He

said, "'If anyone is thirsty, let him come to me and drink. Whoever believes in me, as the Scripture has said, streams of living water will flow from within him'" (John 7:37–38). Jesus offered people what they needed most: a relationship with God. A relationship that is freely given to all who trust in Him. A relationship that satisfies our deepest thirst.

As a follower of Christ, I am committed to living out His teachings and am connected to a church community. So you could say I'm a religious person. But I'd be quick to tell you that it's not religion that quenches my thirsty soul, it's a relationship with Christ. That's what humans really need.

How should those who claim the truth approach others they consider in error? How do you feel about talking to people about the merits of your faith position?

A friend and I met for lunch at a busy neighbourhood restaurant. We quickly agreed to order the salmon and rice. However, the real main course at our table was not the food—it was faith.

You see, my friend and I come from different faith perspectives. We met to talk about the merits of our beliefs. He's convinced all religious roads lead to God. I believe religion can lead to a spiritual dead end. He sees Jesus as one of the ways to get to God, and I believe Jesus was speaking the truth when He said, "'I am the way and the truth and the life. No one comes to the Father except through Me'" (John 14:6).

Our lunchtime conversation was both engaging and earnest. I tried to talk with my friend the way the apostle Paul spoke with religious seekers in ancient

Athens (Acts 17:16–34). When Paul addressed those from other faiths, he showed them genuine respect. He also gave them good reasons for believing that God had revealed Himself in Christ Jesus. Paul sought to be both compassionate and convincing when presenting the case for the uniqueness of Christ.

I count it an honour to talk about Jesus to others from different faith perspectives. We may not always agree, but our conversations need not be disagreeable. My friend and I left the restaurant with a hug and a promise to talk again. We already agree about salmon—one day I hope we'll agree about spirituality.

What are the basic visual identifiers of your religion and their importance to the practice of your faith?

You won't be surprised to hear the cross is the most basic visual identifier for the Christian faith. Churches put crosses on their walls; people wear them around their necks. Crosses are common in our day; they were controversial in Jesus' day.

The cross was Rome's brutal way of executing its most despised criminals. Death on a cross was designed to be excruciating and humiliating. Cicero, the Roman statesman, wrote, "Let the very name of the cross be far, not only from the body of a Roman citizen, but even from his thoughts, his eyes, his ears." [1]

So why would Christians identify themselves with something as demeaning and distasteful as the cross? Why would Paul write, "May I never boast except in the

---

[1] Cicero, *Pro Rabirio.*

cross of our Lord Jesus Christ" (Galatians 6:14)? Why would he say, "we preach Christ crucified" (1 Corinthians 1:23)?

The answer is that the cross proclaims good news for all people. Jesus willingly died to pay for the sins of the whole world—including your sins and mine. "He himself bore our sins in his body on the tree" (1 Peter 2:24). No wonder we call the day Jesus died "Good Friday."

All who embrace the message of the cross, trusting in Jesus' death and resurrection as payment for their sins, are given forgiveness and eternal salvation. "For the message of the cross is foolishness to those who are perishing, but to us who are being saved it is the power of God" (1 Corinthians 1:18).

All religions claim to speak the truth, but they have great differences in their view of reality. Is there such a thing as ultimate truth?

The Christian faith affirms the existence of ultimate truth. By ultimate truth I'm referring to beliefs that accurately correspond to the nature of reality. Some things are absolutely true for all people in all places.

In our postmodern society, the notion of ultimate truth has fallen on hard times. Some have rejected absolute truth, opting for a subjective, relativistic worldview. A friend once told me, "You have your truth and I have mine." He was saying truth is subjectively, not objectively, determined.

The problem with relativism is that it is logically self-defeating. Take the assertion: "Truth is relative." If this statement is correct, then relativism has proven itself false. It's given us an ultimate truth. And that's the one thing it can't do!

But affirming the reality of ultimate truth still leaves us with another question: Can we ultimately know ultimate truth? We are all finite and flawed people. Can we ever hope to know absolute truth in an accurate way?

The Bible says God has made knowing ultimate truth possible. He has revealed truth to us in the Scriptures: "Your word is truth" (John 17:17). He has also revealed truth in His Son, Jesus, who called Himself "the truth" (John 14:6). He promised those who held to His teaching, "you will know the truth and the truth will set you free" (John 8:32).

It's true that we only know ultimate truth "in part" (1 Corinthians 13:12). However, by knowing Jesus we can come to know it in a liberating and life-changing way.

Aside from biblical or scriptural quotations, what does your religion say about life after earthly death?

Answering your question without using a Bible is a bit like playing hockey without a stick. When it comes to formulating our beliefs, Christians should stick to what the Bible teaches. But I'll still take a shot at your question.

If you read literature from the first and second centuries, you'll find that both Jewish and Roman historians (Josephus, Tacitus, Pliny the Younger) make reference to the life and death of Jesus Christ. Some even mention that Jesus' followers were convinced He'd been resurrected. It's a matter of historical record that Christians have always believed Jesus conquered death by rising from the grave.

It shouldn't surprise you, then, that Christians see Jesus as the final authority on life after death. Many religious teachers offer opinions on the matter. But Jesus is unique. He speaks with authority because He personally defeated death.

To learn what Jesus said about life after death, you'll have to open a Bible. If you're worried the Bible won't give you a true rendering of Jesus' words, remember that the Gospels were written before the end of the first century, just several decades after Jesus' death and resurrection. (By contrast, the earliest biography of Alexander the Great was penned 400 years after he died!)

I'd encourage you to take a close look at what Jesus said about life after death. Start by reading John 14. You'll find that Jesus promises all who trust in Him a home in heaven and a life that outlives death.

Does your denomination see Jesus as the only way to God or are there other ways?

Jesus is respected and revered by people of various faiths around the world. Many would agree that He is *a* way to God for some people. But is Jesus the *only* way to God for all people?

Those who are part of our church and denomination believe Jesus is the only way to God. We hold this understanding, knowing that such a view goes against the strong current of religious pluralism in Canada. We hold this view, though many of us have genuine respect for friends from other faiths and religious traditions.

Why do we hold to a view that some would see as intolerant or outdated? Only for one reason: Jesus Himself claimed to be the only way to God. In John 14:6 we read, "Jesus answered, 'I am the way and the truth and the life. No one comes to the Father except through me.'" The apostle Peter echoed this claim in Acts 4:12: "'Salvation is found in no one else, for there is no other name under heaven given to men by which we must be saved.'" These statements lead us to believe that only through trusting in Jesus as Saviour can we come into a personal, saving relationship with God.

The belief that Jesus is the only way to God would be unbelievable if He hadn't done the impossible; His miracles and resurrection from the dead give credibility to His claim. As followers of Jesus, we seek to follow His example and show love and respect for all people. And as believers in Jesus, we also seek to believe His words—even His claim to be the only way to God.

Is envy always bad?

The Bible consistently treats envy as an enemy that should be exiled from our hearts. Envy is a combination of discontent and dislike that leaves us feeling restless inside and resentful of others. If jealousy makes us fearful of losing what we do have, envy makes us spiteful towards those who possess what we don't have (but wish we did).

Not only is envy bad, it's bad to the bone. Proverbs 14:30 says, "envy rots the bones." It eats away at the very core of our lives.

Jesus listed envy as one of the sins that make us dirty inside (see Mark 7:20–23). The apostle Paul identified envy as one of the spiritual toxins that contaminate our hearts (Galatians 5:21).

It's no wonder the Bible calls Christians to get rid of

it: "Therefore, rid yourselves of all malice and all deceit, hypocrisy, envy, and slander of every kind " (1 Peter 2:1).

Envy not only rots our lives, it also ruins our relationships. The Bible makes it plain that love "does not envy" (1 Corinthians 13:4). Envy turns our focus inward (what we want); love directs our focus outward (what another needs). When envy comes in the front door, love goes out the back door.

So what should we do when we are feeling envious? Where do we get the power to defeat the enemy of envy? The Bible says the strength to overcome envy comes from God's Spirit.

When God's Holy Spirit resides in our hearts, He can rescue us from being enslaved to envy. He can fill us with a love strong enough to expel envy every time it enters (Galatians 5:16–26).

How can a person have God's Spirit living inside? In Ephesians 1:13–14, we're told that God sends His Spirit into the life of each person who sincerely trusts in His Son, Jesus.

Is hell a real place where people suffer eternally after death, or is it just a state of mind that changes with a person's mood and circumstances?

For many Canadians today, hell isn't what it used to be. The 1990 Project Canada Survey revealed that only forty-six percent of Canadians believed in a literal hell. Often the word *hell* is used to describe a painful time in this life rather than a painful place in the after-life. People talk about going through hell on earth; they are more reluctant to talk about going to hell after life on earth.

Even those who do agree that hell is an actual place don't seem overly frightened by it. We tend to see hell as it is pictured in Gary Larson's *Far Side* cartoons— more annoying than agonizing, more of a nuisance than a nightmare.

But if we want a realistic understanding of hell, we'll need to listen to the words of Jesus. He had much to say on the topic. His words were striking and sobering. Jesus didn't do a soft sell on hell. He spoke of it as a real place—a place where torment and tears go on forever (Mark 9:42–48).

Some wonder how a loving God could send anyone to a horrific place like hell. The Bible tells us that God doesn't want anyone to perish (2 Peter 3:9). In fact, God has gone to great lengths to save us and spare us from hell. John 3:16 says, "For God so loved the world that he gave his one and only Son, that whoever believes in him shall not perish but have eternal life."

C.S. Lewis once wrote: "There are only two kinds of people in the end: those who say to God, 'Thy will be done,' and those to whom God says in the end, 'Thy will be done.' All that are in hell choose it." [1]

The grim news is that hell is a real place of eternal sorrow. The good news is that God has made a way for all who trust in Jesus to escape hell and enter heaven.

---

[1] C.S. Lewis, *The Great Divide*.

The Bible, the Gospels and the Qur'an are similar in principle but different in their interpretation. Are they to be taken by the letter for eternity, or to be interpreted according to changed times, mores and needs? If so, by whom?

How should the Bible or the Qur'an be interpreted? Do these ancient books still speak to today's needs? Does their interpretation change with changing times? Do they need to be updated or upgraded to be useful in our day? I'll focus my answer on the interpretation of the Bible, since it's the book I base my life upon.

How does one interpret what the Bible is saying? When I read a section of Scripture, I begin by asking, "What did this passage mean to its original readers?" To answer this question, I prayerfully and carefully consider both the text (the words selected in a passage) and the context (the historical setting of the passage). Understanding the original message of the Scripture is what's involved in correctly interpreting the Bible.

But isn't this ancient message out of date in a modern world? Not at all. The Bible is ancient, but its truth is still very applicable. Because God does not change, what the Bible reveals about Him doesn't need to be updated.

Also, since human needs and human nature remain consistent across the centuries, what the Bible says about people still is relevant and reliable. The truth of Scripture is both timeless and timely. Its interpretation has application to various cultures and conditions.

Who is able to interpret and apply the teaching of the Bible? Anyone can (and should) read the Bible, but to fully understand its spiritual truth, you need the help of God's Holy Spirit (1 Corinthians 2:10–16).

Thankfully the Bible promises that God's Spirit comes to live in everyone who sincerely trusts in Jesus for salvation.

Can Satan be forgiven?

The Bible is clear that God forgives sins: "If we confess our sins, he is faithful and just and will forgive us our sins and purify us from all unrighteousness" (1 John 1:9). But does this promise apply to Satan? To answer this question we must know something about forgiveness and something about Satan.

The Bible says forgiveness is a gift; it's a present from God. But like all gifts, to be enjoyed, it must be accepted. How does a person reach out and take God's gift of forgiveness? By humbly trusting in Jesus (Acts 10:43).

This amazing gift of forgiveness is offered to the worst of sinners (1 Timothy 1:15–17). It's offered to all who repent (turn from sin) and believe (turn to Jesus).

So what about Satan? He certainly is sinful. But he also is an angelic being, not a human being. God seems to deal with angels differently than humans. There is no evidence in Scripture that the forgiveness provided by Christ's death on the cross is offered to fallen angels like Satan. There is also no evidence that Satan wants it.

Jesus said Satan is headed for a place designed for him and his angels, a place we call hell (Matthew 25:41, Revelation 20:10). That's bad news for Satan. The good news is that God's gift of forgiveness is available to all people who will reach and receive it by faith.

What is your perspective on the terror caused by the fundamentalists among Muslim clerics and their followers?

There is something terribly twisted about terrorism, especially when it is triggered by religious devotion. A grisly succession of bombings and beheadings has left our world stunned and bleeding. Many of these horrific deeds have been done in the name of God. And to make matters worse, some Muslim clerics have actually tried to give spiritual legitimacy to the brutality. The idea of religious leaders condoning terror is simply beyond belief.

From a Christian perspective, there is never a good reason to resort to terrorism. In many countries around our world, thousands of Christians face daily and deadly persecution. Their only crime is their undying allegiance to Jesus Christ. Yet, instead of resorting to violence when persecuted, these Christians follow the example of Jesus and respond with compassion rather than retaliation. They obey Jesus command to "'Love your enemies and pray for those who persecute you'" (Matthew 5:44). True Christians understand that it may be necessary to die for their faith, but it's never right to kill for it.

All people of faith should be quick to denounce anyone who claims spiritual sanction for terrorism. Religious terrorism is a contradiction in terms. It must not be tolerated.

On the basis that France is a "secular state," French students are restricted from wearing Muslim headscarves, large crucifixes, Jewish men's yarmulkes and other symbols of religion in public schools. What limits, if any, should legislators set in aiding believers and non-believers to live together peaceably in a pluralistic state like Canada?

Recently France made another bold fashion statement. President Jacques Chirac declared that religious wear is officially out of style in France's schools. The government wanted to ban "signs and dress that conspicuously show the religious (faith) of students." Headscarves, skullcaps and large crosses have been expelled from school.

Mr. Chirac says these new limitations will help promote peace in France. Should Canada consider following suit? I don't think so. Here's why.

Peace among people requires changing hearts, not just changing clothes. Imagine that Canada decided to prohibit people from wearing sportswear supporting their favourite hockey team. No more Maple Leaf jerseys. No more Sens sweatshirts. Would this law lead to greater goodwill between hockey fans? No, because uniformity is not the same thing as unity.

Peace among people requires more respect, not more restrictions. Laws are already in place to punish those who would break the peace. Those who do violence, even in the name of religion, should be punished. Limiting religious attire is both unfair and unnecessary.

For Christians, the cross is not just a fashion accessory. It's our hope for peace. The Bible says Jesus came "to reconcile to himself all things, whether things on earth or things in heaven, by making peace through his blood" (Colossians 1:20). Through faith in Christ's death and resurrection, we gain peace with God and a basis for making peace with others.

What does your faith teach about substance abuse, and how should society help those who are dealing with various addictions?

The Christian faith offers great hope and help to those struggling with addictions. Christians follow the example of Jesus, who compassionately cared for the hurting (Matthew 9:12). We seek to provide people with a safe place to change and point them to God's supernatural power for change.

To break free from addictions, we need a safe place to change. We need a community that offers us both love (which comforts) and truth (which confronts). Over the years Christians have established numerous clinics for those stuck in a lifestyle of substance abuse. Many churches invite people into recovery groups where supportive friendships are developed.

To move towards true freedom, people need more than a safe place. They also need supernatural power.

The folks at AA understand this. They encourage participants to look to a "higher power" for help. Christians know that the name of the "higher power" is Jesus. Listen to the hope and help Jesus offers: "'If you hold to my teaching, you are really my disciples. Then you will know the truth, and the truth will set you free'" (John 9:31–32).

A safe place and God's supernatural power will only help those with a strong desire to change. Jesus once asked a man who'd been debilitated for decades, "'Do you want to get well?'" (John 5:6). That's the sobering question each person must answer. Those who come to Jesus with a passion to change discover He has the power to grant forgiveness and guide them towards true freedom.

Does your religion have theological or other objections to the celebration of Halloween?

Halloween is a holiday that wears a mask. On one level, it's about children dressed as clowns or cowboys collecting enough candy to scare a dentist. But, behind Halloween's harmless disguise is a darker side.

Halloween is historically linked to fears about wandering spirits and evil omens. Over the years, the holiday has continued to be associated with witchcraft and the demonic.

Though some in North America dismiss the notion of demons, the Bible does not. It tells us of a spiritual realm that is unseen but not unreal. It warns to steer clear of the devil and his demonic cohorts since they are deceptive and destructive (2 Corinthians 11:14; John 8:44). Dressing up as a devil or a witch on Halloween only glamorizes or trivializes what the Bible calls demonic.

Christians don't have to be frightened on Halloween. While demonic beings are powerful, they have been defeated. When Jesus died on the cross, He not only provided forgiveness for all who believe but also disarmed demonic powers. Colossians 2:15 proclaims that Jesus "disarmed the powers and authorities...triumphing over them by the cross." Those who trust in Jesus can "be strong in the Lord and in power of his might" (Ephesians 6:10).

So how should Christians respond? Some will choose to sit out any celebration of Halloween. Others will find ways for their kids to enjoy candy and costumes without dabbling in the darkness. Increasingly, churches are offering fun-filled alternatives on Halloween night where kids can get treats without being tricked.

Do you believe, as some TV evangelists have suggested, that civil liberties groups, feminists, homosexuals and abortion rights supporters bear partial responsibility for the terrorist attacks in the U.S. because they have turned God against America? If not, how could God have allowed such terrible things to happen?

When the twin towers fell down in New York, they raised up an old question: Why does God allow such terrible things to happen? While a complete answer is beyond our reach, the Bible points to two truths that help explain the existence of evil in our world: our freedom and our fallenness.

When God created humans, He gave us the freedom to make choices (Genesis 2:17). He could have designed us as programmable robots, but He desired that we choose a personal relationship with Him. So God gave us freedom—freedom to choose His way or our own way, freedom to say "Thy will be done" or "My will be done."

In Genesis 3, you can read how our first parents misused their freedom and disobeyed God. In the newspaper you can read how people today still abuse freedom and choose to do things that grieve and anger God. In our fallen world, some use their freedom to cause terror and create tragedy. Our freedom makes evil possible. Our fallenness makes evil pervasive.

What about the claim that God is allowing evil to erupt in America because He is angered by the sins of certain groups or individuals? While the Bible does warn that God will judge sin in both nations and in individuals, it also makes it clear that all of us qualify as sinners. The Old Testament says, "We all, like sheep, have gone astray" (Isaiah 53:6). The New Testament echoes, "All have sinned and fall short of the glory of God" (Romans 3:23).

The *Times of London* once asked a number of writers to compose essays on the topic "What's Wrong with the World?" G.K. Chesterton's article was short and straightforward. He replied, "Dear Sirs: I am." Chesterton understood that each of us is a sinner in need of God's grace.

At this time of tragedy, we should choose to humble our own hearts, repent of our own sins and trust in Christ for forgiveness and mercy. Now is not the time to be pointing our fingers at others. Now is the time to be bending our knees before God.

With so many different versions of the Bible and other scriptures available, how can people decide which they should read and whether it is truly the Word of God?

How can a person know whether the Bible is really the Word of God? 2 Timothy 3:16 says: "All scripture is God-breathed and is useful for teaching, rebuking, correcting and training in righteousness." The Bible claims its words were breathed out by God before they were written down by humans. Any book can claim to be from God. But the Bible is unique. Its credibility backs up its claim.

First, the Bible has proven historically reliable. Archeological discoveries have consistently confirmed the Bible's historical credibility. Archeologist Nelson Glueck wrote, "It may be stated categorically that no archeological discovery has ever controverted a biblical reference."[1] Since the Bible has proven true in areas we can test empirically (matters of history), we have good reason to trust it where we can't easily test it (matters of faith).

Second, the Bible has proven prophetically accurate. For example, the exact city where Jesus would be born was predicted over 600 years before His birth (Micah 5:2).

Third, the Bible has been globally influential. The message of the Bible has changed the lives of people from all cultures in all times and all places. I'm an example; the good news of salvation through faith in Jesus has transformed my life.

Your second question asks which version of the Bible to read. Select a version that's translated from ancient Hebrew and Greek manuscripts, such as the New International Version or the New King James Version. I'd encourage you to get into the Bible (beginning with the New Testament) and let its life-changing message get into you.

---

1 Nelson Glueck, *Rivers in the Desert.*

Aside from the Scriptures of your faith, what evidence would you cite for the existence of God?

If you are looking for evidences that God exists, here are two things worth looking at. First, check out the creation around you.

When an anthropologist finds a small, triangular-shaped rock, he looks for clues to determine whether the rock is shaped that way through natural causes (such as erosion) or intelligent causes (someone making an arrowhead).

Use that same logic when you look at our world. Examine the incredible complexity of the cell. Consider the organs in the human body or the orbits of the heavenly bodies. Ask yourself, "Do I think all this is the result of natural causes (chance and time) or an intelligent cause (a Creator)?" It seems logical to me that the intricate designs in creation point to the existence of an intelligent Designer.

As the second evidence, I'd ask you to listen to your conscience.

In his book *Mere Christianity*, C.S. Lewis points out that humans "have this curious idea that they ought to behave in a certain way, and cannot really get rid of it."[1] Lewis makes a strong case that this internal moral law argues for an external Lawgiver of some kind.

Creation and conscience point to the existence of a Creator. They clue us in to the fact that God is, but don't tell us much about what God is like. That's where Jesus comes in. The Bible says He came to make the invisible God visible. Creation and conscience evidence the existence of God. Jesus embodies the essence of God.

---

[1] C.S. Lewis, *Mere Christianity*.

Should religion play a part in our federal elections?

If you wonder whether religion should play a part in the next election, ask yourself this question: Should values play a part in our federal elections? Most people would agree values should play a part in politics. We want politicians to be value-driven, not just vote-driven. We want them to be people of principle, not simply political pragmatists.

Values also shape the way we vote in an election. Our personal convictions affect our political decisions. Our beliefs influence the way we mark our ballots. If it's true that values should play a part in an election, then it follows that religion should, too. After all, religious teachings shape the personal values of many Canadians. For example, the teachings of Jesus give me a solid, unchanging basis for determining what is right, good and desirable. My faith in Christ shapes my outlook on life.

To try to exclude religion from playing a part in the upcoming election is not only impossible—it's intolerant. Religion isn't the only voice that shapes values. Family, friends, media and even political action groups all seek to influence what we consider important. We don't try to silence them during an election campaign. So why single out religion?

While it's true that churches are not to endorse specific candidates or political parties, they have a right and a responsibility to teach values. And those values will influence how people vote. In fact, if your faith doesn't shape your values, you don't value your faith.

Should politicians and judges be allowed to display Scriptures such as the Ten Commandments in government buildings or courts to show people the origin of our laws?

The Ten Commandments may be God's laws, but it's against the law to display them in a government building. That's what Roy Moore, Alabama's Chief Justice, found out. His monument of the Ten Commandments was officially removed from the rotunda of the state's judicial building. A United States district judge ruled that the monument was "nothing less than an obtrusive year-round religious display" and ordered it taken out.

Those opposed to the display cite the need to separate church and state. But, in doing so, they also separate a nation from its history. Historically, the Ten Commandments helped shape the legal codes in the United States and Canada. Normally, a nation's heritage is something to be commemorated, even celebrated. Evidently, that's not the case if that heritage is religious.

To deny that the Ten Commandments are part of God's law is a personal decision; to deny that they are part of our heritage is a historical revision.

Visitors to the Canadian Parliament buildings are reminded that our country has a history shaped by Scripture. Carved in stone on the Peace Tower are the words of Psalm 72:8, "He shall have dominion from sea to sea" (KJV).

This verse inspired Sir Leonard Tilley, one of our founding fathers, to propose that the name of our country be the Dominion of Canada. So, Psalm 72:8 is carved into our nation's history. Displaying these words on a government building may not be considered politically correct, but it is certainly historically accurate.

What does your faith teach about the death penalty?

John Grisham's novel *The Chamber* captures the controversy that surrounds the death penalty. When a convicted killer, Sam Cayhall, is sentenced to the gas chamber, the community divides and debates the morality of putting him to death.

Christians approach this difficult issue with a conviction that God is ultimately the giver and taker of life. He controls the beginning and ending of each of our lives.

God has allowed humans to play a part in His creation of life through procreation. So does He also give us a role to play in the termination of life? Here's where evangelical Christians have some honest differences.

We all agree that God forbids murder. Individuals must not take vengeance by taking another life.

We also agree that God has commissioned governments with the responsibility of protecting the innocent and punishing the guilty. Romans 13:4 says a ruler is "God's servant to do you good. But if you do wrong, be afraid, for he does not bear the sword for nothing. He is God's servant, an agent of wrath to bring punishment on the wrongdoer."

Some evangelicals understand this verse to allow governments to execute justice even when it means executing convicted killers. They point out that "bearing the sword" seems to imply more than simply locking someone up for a long time. Others would contend that governments can punish wrongdoers without resorting to the death penalty.

Even though Christians come to different conclusions in the death penalty debate, we are united in proclaiming God's offer of eternal life to all who trust in Jesus for forgiveness. Even those on death row.

Are there saints in your religion who are teachers by example or are saints regarded as intermediaries between believers and God?

All true Christians are saints. I know that sounds a bit over the top. But that's what the Bible calls people who've become followers of Jesus. The New Testament book of Romans is addressed to "all in Rome who are loved by God and called to be saints." Ephesians is written to "the saints in Ephesus."

How can all Christians be saints when they don't always act saintly? Well, the word *saints* literally means *holy ones*. All who've put their faith in Jesus are considered holy ones in God's eyes. They've become new creations (2 Corinthians 5:17) and have begun to be renewed from the inside out.

If those who trust in Jesus are saints, does this mean they should be teachers by example? It sure does. Christian leaders are told to be examples for the whole church (1 Peter 5:3). Even younger Christians are to set "an example by doing what is good" (Titus 2:7). That's a high calling, but an essential one. A mark of a true Christian is a changed life.

Do some Christians become so "saintly" that they are intermediaries between other believers and God? The Bible teaches there is only "one mediator between God and men, the man Christ Jesus" (1 Timothy 2:5). Jesus said, "No one comes to the Father except through me " (John 14:6). If you want to come close to God, you don't have to go through any other human. You can connect with God directly through faith in Christ.

What part does faith play in the preservation of our cultural heritage?

The Christian faith plays a part in preserving the cultural heritage of people around the world. But it does much more than that. It also transcends and transforms cultures.

Christianity is embraced by people from all cultures. I'm reminded of that every Sunday morning. One of the things I like best about the church I pastor is its cultural diversity. The last time we counted, over thirty languages were spoken by the people in the church. What binds us together is not our cultural backgrounds, but our belief in Jesus. As Galatians 3:28 explains, "There is neither Jew nor Greek...for you are all one in Christ Jesus." Christianity transcends culture.

The Christian faith not only connects cultures, it also corrects them. All cultures, like all people, have flaws.

Selfishness and sensuality creep in and cause moral and spiritual corrosion. The Bible gives a transcultural basis for bringing cultures back in line with God's design. So Christianity transforms culture.

The Christian faith also preserves cultural diversity. In the book of Revelation, the apostle John is given a vision of heaven. He sees "a great multitude that no one could count, from every nation, tribe, people and language" (Revelation 7:9). Even in heaven, we will still have our cultural colourings. God finds beauty in the mosaic of peoples He has made.

That's why He offers eternal life to people from all cultures who will simply and sincerely place their faith in Jesus.

What special knowledge did the prophets in your faith have about the past, present and future? If they did have knowledge of the future, why did they not tell people specifically what would happen and when?

The Christian faith not only explains the past and makes sense of the present, it also predicts the future. Biblical prophets predicted future events with amazing precision.

The prophet Isaiah accurately foretold the name of a Persian ruler, Cyrus, a century before he was born (Isaiah 44:28). The prophet Daniel correctly predicted that Babylonia, Persia, Greece and Rome would be the next four world powers (Daniel 2 and 7).

Six hundred years before Jesus was born, Isaiah foresaw His virgin birth (Isaiah 7:14). Also, six centuries before Christ, the prophet Micah announced that the Messiah would be born in the tiny town of Bethlehem (Micah 5:2).

Isaiah predicted God's Suffering Servant would be "pierced" for the sins of others (Isaiah 53:5). The prophet Zechariah even specified that His hands and feet would be pierced (Zechariah 12:10). These predictions are even more stunning when you realize that crucifixion was not commonly practiced until centuries later, during the time of Christ.

Some of the events that biblical prophets spoke about are still in the future. In the book of Revelation, we're told a climactic, global battle will take place in Israel, in the valley of Megiddo or Armageddon (Revelation 16:16). Afterwards, Jesus will return to judge and rule the earth.

Biblical prophets made their predictions not simply to satisfy our curiosity, but to substantiate our faith. Since the prophets have proven so accurate in the past, we have good reason to believe what they say about our future will come true as well.

What should churches, mosques and synagogues do to attract people turned off by organized religion?

Last week I had breakfast in a restaurant that attracts and packs in people. While some restaurants in our city are almost empty, folks stand in line to get a seat in this place. Why?

Well, the atmosphere is pleasing, the servers are pleasant, but I think the main reason people come (and come back) is because the food is fabulous. You always leave having been well fed. Your hunger has been satisfied.

I realize that this week's question is about religion, not restaurants. But I see some parallels that help me answer the question of how churches can attract people.

God created people with a spiritual hunger that is as real as physical hunger. Our hearts, not just our stomachs, need to be filled. We crave a sense of God's close-ness and care.

Our souls get famished and malnourished when we feed them only the cotton-candy pleasures of life. We long for something that has spiritual substance. We want to be satisfied.

As a pastor I'm convinced that hungry hearts find substance and satisfaction in a relationship with Jesus. It was Jesus who said, "If anyone is thirsty, let him come to me and drink" (John 7:37). The Bible invites all who are spiritually hungry to "taste and see that the LORD is good" (Psalm 34:8).

When people come to a church where they sense the reality of Christ, their hearts begin to salivate. They come back for more. And they tell their friends. I grew up in a church whose motto was "the place where hungry hearts are fed." I'd stand in line to get a seat in a church like that.

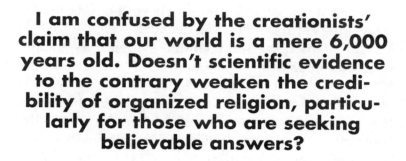

I am confused by the creationists' claim that our world is a mere 6,000 years old. Doesn't scientific evidence to the contrary weaken the credibility of organized religion, particularly for those who are seeking believable answers?

The age of Earth is an age-old question. Some scientists claim our planet is billions of years old; other scientists contend it's considerably younger. Back in the seventeenth century, Bishop James Usher calculated the number of years in the genealogical records listed in the book of Genesis: He concluded that Earth is only 6,000 years old.

The scientific data about the age of our world is still being debated. A variety of scientific observations have been made that fit well with the young earth scenario (for example, the earth's decaying magnetic field, the shrinking size of our sun, the drift of the moon away from the earth, etc.) Further, those who argue that certain fossils or rocks are millions of years old use a method of geological dating that seems far more speculative than scientific. Radiometric dating is far from reliable, being based on a number of unproven assumptions about our earth's past. In short, the data for the date of the earth is still being debated.

Christians don't see scientific evidence as antagonistic to our faith in Christ and our confidence in the Bible. Instead, we see true science as an ally. What is observed in nature argues forcefully against the notion that our world is the product of random chance. On the contrary, a wide range of scientific discoveries (from the orbits of heavenly bodies to the organs of human bodies) support the biblical concept of special creation.

Biochemists such as Michael Behe (see his book, *Darwin's' Black Box*[1]) are convinced the intricacies of the cell's design points to an Intelligent Designer. And the opening verse in the Bible introduces us to that Intelligent Designer: "In the beginning God created the heavens and the earth" (Genesis 1:1).

While the Bible doesn't give an exact age for the earth, it does give us something better. It tells us through faith in Christ, we can come to personally know our Creator.

---

[1] Michael Behe, *Darwin's Black Box*.

In the book of Joshua, the Israelites are commanded by God to invade the land across the Jordan River that became Israel and to wipe out certain segments of the population. How can a loving God order His chosen people to do such things in His name?

How could a loving God order a large-scale destruction of Canaanite society? Why would He order Joshua to wipe out the inhabitants of entire cities like Jericho or Ai? For years, this question has been asked by both seekers and skeptics.

This isn't the only time the Bible speaks of God bringing severe judgment on large populations. He poured out the flood on the earth in Noah's day (Genesis 6), rained down fire from heaven on Sodom and Gomorrah in Abraham's time (Genesis 19) and sent a deadly plague on Israel in David's day (2 Samuel 24).

In the New Testament, Revelation warns that God will send unparalleled devastation in the last days.

How can a loving God act in such lethal ways? The Bible answers that God is loving, but also holy and just. Because He is loving, He is slow to anger (Psalm 103:8); because He is holy, His patience has a limit (Nehemiah 9:30). He will judge those who persist in resisting His will and rejecting His ways. That's what the Canaanites did. Their society became known for malignant immorality and child sacrifices. God patiently gave them time to change. Genesis 15:16 indicates that God delayed judgment for four generations. But, finally, time ran out and God's judgment came in the form of Joshua's armies (Joshua 6:17–19).

The question that lingers in my mind is not "How can a loving God judge sinful people?" but rather, "How can a holy God love sinful people?"

None of us is righteous before Him (Romans 3:9–12). The Bible makes it clear that all of us deserve judgment for our sins. Yet in His great love, God sent His Son, Jesus, to take the judgment we deserved. Now He graciously and patiently gives us time to turn from our sin, trust in Christ and avoid His judgment. As 2 Peter 3:9 says, "He is patient with you, not wanting anyone to perish, but everyone to come to repentance."

Why did God create an immortal Satan as an archenemy?

In J.R.R. Tolkien's trilogy, *The Lord Of The Rings*, the inhabitants of Middle Earth live under the shadow of the Dark Lord, Sauron. His lust for the Ring and its power brings suffering and death to many. While Tolkien's story of Middle Earth is fictional, it's not completely fanciful. There is a Dark Lord—Satan. His lust for power has caused great devastation and death on planet Earth.

The Bible tells us that Satan was not originally God's archenemy but one of God's archangels. Like the other angelic beings, he was created to worship and serve his Creator. But being filled with pride, he rebelled against God (1Timothy 3:6). Satan was created good, but he became evil.

If God made Satan to be good, why did He allow

him to go bad? Perhaps for the same reason He lets humans go bad. God desires that His creatures respond to Him with a love that is free and not forced. Satan abused his freedom and become a slave of evil.

After allowing Satan to go bad, why does God allow him to go on? Why not stop his malicious and malignant actions? The Bible says God will do just that. Revelation 20:10 tells us that one day God will throw Satan into a lake of burning sulphur to be tormented day and night forever. Satan's time is limited, his doom is certain and his punishment will be eternal.

While Satan has become God's enemy, he has never been God's equal. For that reason, we need not live in fear of Satan's power. Instead, we should follow the admonition given in James 4:7–8: "Submit yourselves, then, to God. Resist the devil, and he will flee from you. Come near to God and He will come near to you."

As we come near to God by trusting in His Son, Jesus, we can experience victory over God's archenemy.

A leading clergyman has stated that the Bible is not for children, filled as it is with sex and violence. What is your reaction?

Keeping the Bible from children would be a childish mistake. It is true that when children read the Bible they will learn about our human failings, including the sins of immorality and violence.

However, unlike many books children read, the Bible does not sensationalize sexual sin or glamorize gore. Instead, a moral framework undergirds the discussion of human immorality and inhumanity. The Bible does not confuse kids with a worldview that blurs the distinction between right and wrong. In a day when many children are morally unfocused, the Bible can help bring clarity to their personal convictions.

But the Bible goes further than just helping children grow towards moral maturity; it also points them towards spiritual salvation. That's why the apostle Paul could remind his young apprentice Timothy to:

> Continue in what you have learned and have become convinced of, because you know those from whom you learned it, and how from infancy you have known the holy Scriptures, which are able to make you wise for salvation through faith in Christ Jesus (2 Timothy 3:14–15).

Timothy's mother and grandmother taught him the Scriptures "from infancy." As a child he learned the truth about salvation through faith in Jesus.

I'm glad the Scriptures were not withheld from me as a child. And I can't imagine keeping God's book away from the children God loves so much. After all, it was Jesus who said, "'I tell you the truth, unless you change and become like little children, you will never enter the kingdom of heaven'" (Matthew 18:3).

One is never too young to learn what the Bible says about having childlike faith in Christ.

Every faith includes teachings on what adherents must do, whether it is on ethical issues such as abortion, or religious practices such as worship. What would you estimate as the percentage of your faith's adherents who wholeheartedly follow those teachings? How important is it that they do so?

How important is it that Christians wholeheartedly follow the teachings of Christ? Extremely important. Jesus made that clear. In His final instructions He said, "Go and make disciples of all nations, baptizing them in the name of the Father and of the Son and of the Holy Spirit, and teaching them to obey everything I have commanded you" (Matthew 28:19–20). He wants His followers to obey "everything" He commanded.

So how many Christians wholeheartedly follow Christ's teaching? That's tough to estimate. Here's why. A person becomes a Christian when he trusts in Jesus as his only hope to be forgiven and given eternal life (John 5:24). The moment he believes, God moves into his life; his heart becomes the Holy Spirit's home (Ephesians 1:13–14). The Holy Spirit goes to work to remodel the Christian's character and conduct. That involves a major renovation, and it takes time.

Every Christian is a work in progress. The more we co-operate through our faith and obedience, the faster change takes place. But the full internal makeover won't be finished until we arrive in heaven. As Philippians 1:6 promises, "He who began a good work in you will carry it on to completion until the day of Christ Jesus."

Until that time, those of us who know and love Jesus won't evidence perfection. But we should show progress. If we truly belong to Christ, we will grow to look more and more like Him in our attitudes and actions.

How should we pray, and is prayer still relevant today?

Asking how to pray puts you in good company. One of Jesus' first disciples had the same request: "'Lord, teach us to pray'" (Luke 11:1). Jesus answered by giving His followers a pattern for prayer. We know it as the Lord's Prayer—the familiar prayer that begins, "Our Father who art in heaven..."

Many people think the Lord's Prayer is just for reciting in church. But it's more than that. The Lord's Prayer gives us a blueprint for our everyday prayers. It gives us topics for talking to God.

The Lord's Prayer begins by reminding us to pray about God's concerns. We ask that His name would be honoured. We pray that His kingdom (his rule) would spread on earth. We pray that His will would be done in our lives and our land. Talking to God about these requests keeps our prayers from becoming small and self-centred.

But Jesus also invites us to pray about our own needs. We pray for daily bread—the things we need to live. We ask for forgiveness and promise to forgive others. We appeal for spiritual protection, both for ourselves and for those we love.

To really pray effectively we need a family relationship with God. Notice the Lord's Prayer begins with the words, "Our Father." To have God as our Father, we must trust His Son, Jesus, as our Saviour.

How long will this kind of prayer be relevant? As long as we have needs. That means as long as we live!

Do you believe there are really angels, or do you think that people who believe in them are engaging in wishful thinking about supernatural guidance and protection?

Angels are soaring in popularity these days. They get primetime airtime on TV. They're good as gold in jewellery stores. They're really *in*. But are they real?

The Bible's answer is that angels really do exist. Angels are mentioned in thirty-four of the Bible's sixty-six books. Jesus repeatedly referred to them. When it comes to angels, unseen doesn't mean unreal.

Though angels do exist, many of the popular notions about them are wishful thinking. Our culture sells us a Disney version of angels that portrays them as spiritual Tinkerbells. Angels are supposedly cute and cuddly, helpful but harmless.

But this view of angels doesn't fly with the Bible. The Bible informs us that angels are powerful, spiritual beings. People who encounter them are usually terrified or awestruck. The soldiers guarding Jesus' tomb collapsed in fear when an angel came down to announce that Jesus had risen (Matthew 28:4).

Do angels provide supernatural guidance and protection? The Bible does tell us of times when God dispatched angels to deliver a message or deliver someone in trouble. But we're never told to ask angels for direction or protection; we are to call on God for help. In fact, the Bible warns us that fallen angels, called demons, will seek to deceive and destroy us.

So, impressive as angels can be, they are not to occupy our attention or affection. We're not to worship them (Colossians 2:18–19). Rather, we are to join them in worshipping God and His Son, Jesus (Revelation 5:11–14).

What is your faith's perspective on the relationship between ecology and spirituality?

Imagine a close friend just built a waterfront home in the Muskokas. And suppose he gave you the house keys for an extended stay. How would you treat his place? Would you trash it or take care of it?

The Bible says God built a breathtakingly beautiful world. Genesis 1:1 declares, "In the beginning God created the heavens and the earth." To cap off His creative work, God made humans and told us to take dominion over all of His creation (Genesis 1:28; 2:15). You might say He gave us the keys to His place.

Should we trash it or take care of it? The answer is clear. If we love and reverence our Creator, we will govern and guard His creation. Christian spirituality leads to a concern for ecology.

But even though the earth is made by God, it isn't divine. So while we are to watch over the earth, we aren't to worship it. In fact, one of the indicators of spirituality gone bad is that people worship "created things rather than the Creator" (Romans 1:25). Worship is only to be given to God through His Son, Jesus.

The earth is a wonderful place to live. But it belongs to God (Psalm 24:1). So we should take care of it in a way that shows our love and respect for Him.

What are the pitfalls of your faith, and how can religious leaders lead believers into a deeper grasp of their faith?

The pitfalls of the Christian faith have to do with Christians, rather than our faith. I've been a follower of Christ for forty years now. I've not uncovered problems with the Christian faith; I have encountered problems with Christian people. While our faith is "most holy" (Jude 1:20), Christians often are not.

One pitfall Christians fall into is taking God's grace for granted. Grace is a distinctive aspect of our faith. Most religions teach that God deals with people based on their goodness—do good things for God and you'll get on good terms with God. Christianity says no one is good enough for God. Salvation comes by God's grace, not human goodness. "For it is by grace you have been saved, through faith—and this is not from yourselves, it is the gift of God—not by works, so that no one can boast" (Ephesians 2:8–9). Christians are people who have received God's saving grace by putting their faith in Jesus.

Here's where a pitfall shows up. Some Christians not only take God's grace for salvation, they also take it for granted. They become careless and casual. They forget that grace "teaches us to say 'No' to ungodliness and worldly passions, and to live self-controlled, upright and godly lives" (Titus 2:12).

As a pastor, I seek to help Christians gain a deeper grasp of their faith by teaching them the truth of the Bible. My job is help them grow in grace (2 Peter 3:18). Growing in grace will keep one from falling into the pits.

What difference do prayer, meditation and other regular spiritual practice make in people's lives?

Spiritual practices can make a big difference in a person's life. I say that from personal experience. For many years I've begun the day with a time of Bible reading and prayer. What a difference it has made!

Taking time to reflectively read a section of Scripture strengthens my heart. It's amazing how often God uses His Word to speak to my life, providing needed correction or direction. Truly, the "word of God is living and active" (Hebrews 4:12).

My heart is also strengthened as I pour it out to God in prayer. God invites us to talk to Him about what's on our hearts. It gives me great comfort to know that God cares deeply. It also gives me great courage to know that God controls supremely. In praying to Him, I'm talking to the One who can answer my prayers wonderfully and wisely.

While it's true that Scripture reading and prayer make a big difference for me, it's also true that they make a difference to God. These regular spiritual practices not only strengthen my heart, they also delight His heart. The Bible says that God made us for a relationship with Himself. Even after we turned our backs on Him, He still loved us. Loved us enough to offer forgiveness and friendship to all who put their faith in His Son, Jesus.

God's passionate pursuit of a relationship with us means He is delighted when we draw near to Him. So, spiritual practices like reading the Bible and praying not only bring us stability, they bring God satisfaction. And that makes a big difference.

Some famous athletes pray to God before competing. Does this give them an edge, or are there some other benefits to prayer before a competition?

At the Sydney Olympics, a Christian athlete who won a gold medal in platform diving said she prayed before each of her dives. Did her prayers play a part in her gold medal performance? Should athletes pray before they play? Does God really care about sporting events?

The Bible points us to some answers for these questions. First, it affirms that Christians, including Christian athletes, should "pray continually" (1 Thessalonians 5:17). God instructs His people to pray when they are anxious (Philippians 4:6). So athletes, who know all about anxiety, can express their hearts to God.

But does praying give them a competitive edge or some other tangible benefit? I believe prayer does have great benefit. God promises to bring peace to our hearts when we pray (Philippians 4:7). That peace can help anxious athletes do their best, whether or not they win the competition.

But the true benefit of prayer for a Christian athlete is a spiritual one. Prayer doesn't ensure an athlete will dominate a sporting competition, but it does ensure he or she will develop a spiritual communion with God. Closeness with God is much more lasting and satisfying than any athletic success (or any other kind of success).

And the good news is that God invites all of us, not just winners and world-class athletes, to enter into a close relationship with Him by trusting in His Son, Jesus. That relationship is only a prayer away.

Is it necessary to believe in a religion to be happy?

For most people, happiness in life is closely linked to what's happening in life. When things are going well, they are doing well. When life is good, they feel happy—whether they are religious or not.

But life isn't a continual good time. Hard times hit us all. And when that happens, most of us don't feel happy—whether we're religious or not. Being religious doesn't shield a person from sorrow.

Jesus knew we'd face troubles that would weigh us down. That's why He said, "'I have told you these things, so that in me you may have peace. In this world you will have trouble. But take heart! I have overcome the world'" (John 16:33). Though life won't be free from trouble, Jesus says it can be full of peace. The peace He gives can stabilize and strengthen us, even when our hearts are heavy.

Jesus also spoke of happiness that's out of this world. He promised those who believe in Him a place in heaven. "'Do not let your hearts be troubled. Trust in God; trust also in me. In my Father's house are many rooms...I am going there to prepare a place for you'" (John 14:1–2). The Bible tells us that in heaven "there will be no more death or mourning or crying or pain" (Revelation 21:4). Now that's a happy ending.

If God asked you whether a saviour or a great prophet should be sent to Earth today or in 100 years, how would you respond?

Without hesitation, I would respond, "Send the Saviour." I would echo the words that the apostle John used to conclude the book of Revelation: "Come, Lord Jesus" (Revelation 22:20).

The Bible promises that Jesus will be sent back to the earth. He came 2,000 years ago to die for our sins. The Bible says "He will appear a second time, not to bear sin, but to bring salvation to those who are waiting for him" (Hebrews 9:28).

When Jesus does return, it will be an earth-shaking event. He made that clear when His disciples asked about His second coming. He predicted famines, earthquakes and wars would shake the world. Wickedness would be on the rise. Many would become spiritually complacent or confused. Then, in the midst of the gathering darkness, He said He would come in power and great glory. He promised to return to rescue those who love Him, recompense those who reject Him and to rule the earth (Matthew 24:1–35).

Should God wait 100 years before sending Jesus? Christians are ready for Jesus to return now. We join John in saying, "Come, Lord Jesus." Yet, there is a good reason why Jesus has not come back yet. God is giving people time to get right with Him. As 2 Peter 3:9 says, "The Lord is not slow in keeping his promise, as some understand slowness. He is patient with you, not wanting anyone to perish, but everyone to come to repentance."

What weight should believers give to their personal religious experiences, as opposed to Scriptures and other means of understanding God and His purpose for us?

Have you ever misjudged someone? Perhaps you had an experience that led you to make an assessment about a person. You drew some conclusions. But later, after he revealed his heart, you came to realize your impressions had been inaccurate. You didn't have all the facts. Your conclusions had been wrong.

If we can be wrong about people, it stands to reason that we can be wrong about God. We can draw conclusions about God that turn out to be mistaken.

That's why personal, religious experiences are not infallible guides when it comes to understanding God and His purposes. That's why the Scriptures are essential. In the Bible, God reveals His heart and His desires.

But God went further than just giving us a book about Himself. He also sent us Jesus. Jesus lets us see

God in flesh and blood. God's self-revelation in the Bible and in Jesus gives us an accurate understanding of what He's like and what He wants.

Does this mean all personal experience of God is extraneous and erroneous? Not at all. We can experience God in a daily, life-shaping way. We can receive a changed heart and a new start as we trust in Jesus. We encounter God as we read the Bible and converse with Him in prayer. We sense His love in our hearts. We see His hand on our lives. Experience can be both personal and powerful. But to be reliable, experience must be governed and guided by God's Word.

How do you react to the U.S. initiative to ban partial-birth abortion, in which a fetus is partially delivered before being killed?

It's hard to be impartial about partial-birth abortions. The actual procedure is so grisly I cannot understand how civilized people can defend it.

The doctor takes forceps and begins a breech delivery. Legs and torso emerge from the womb. The head, with fully formed eyes, eyebrows and eyelashes, remains inside the mother. Then, using scissors or a trochar, the doctor punctures the back of the skull. A suction curette is inserted into the head to vacuum out the brains. The beating heart stops. Life is violently turned to death.

How could an impartial person not be outraged by that?

How could such a practice not be wholly condemned? Only an unconditional commitment to freedom of choice could allow a nation to legalize such a barbaric assault on the smallest and most vulnerable among us.

Jesus gave us a golden guideline for treating people when He said, "So in everything, do to others what you would have them do to you" (Matthew 7:12). Jesus' words call us to care for any woman in the midst of a crisis pregnancy. We should offer her the help we'd want if in her place. But Jesus' words also call us to treat the newborn as if we were in its vulnerable position.

If we want to maintain our reputation as a compassionate people, we must have a Canadian initiative to stop this horrific procedure. Banning partial-birth abortions is a partial step in the right direction.

Catholics and Protestants differ in their approach to prayer, primarily over Catholics' belief that they may not only pray to God, but can also ask Jesus' friends, saints whom the church believes are in heaven, to speak a word to God on their behalf. What does your faith teach about the possibility of receiving divine favours by spoken or silent prayers?

Christians have good reason to believe in the power of prayer. We know from the Bible and from experience that God answers prayer. What kind of prayers does He answer favourably? Whether spoken or silent, the Bible tells us God is looking for certain things in our prayers.

God wants our prayers to be filled with faith. Jesus said, "'Therefore I tell you, whatever you ask for in prayer, believe that you have received it, and it will be yours'" (Mark 11:24)

God also wants our prayers to be backed by obedience. Jesus declared, "'If you remain in me and my words remain in you, ask whatever you wish, and it will be given you'" (John 15:7) We shouldn't expect God to give us what we want when we're not doing what He wants.

Finally, God wants us to pray "in Jesus' name." Jesus taught us, "'And I will do whatever you ask in my name, so that the Son may bring glory to the Father'" (John 14:13)

What does it mean to pray in Jesus' name? It means our requests must be ones Jesus would support. We need to ask ourselves, would Jesus want His name linked to this request?

To pray "in Jesus' name" also means we bring our requests to God based on our relationship with Christ. We don't approach God through saints but rather through His Son (John 14:6; 1 Timothy 2:5). God listens to the prayers of those who are linked to Jesus through faith.

What does your religion believe happens to people at death? Is there an immediate afterlife—either heaven or hell—or do we wait for an indefinite period for reward or punishment?

In the late nineteenth century, a famous Christian leader named Dwight Moody said, "Some day you'll read in the papers that D.L. Moody is dead. Don't you believe a word of it! At that moment I will be more alive than I am right now. I shall have gone up higher, that is all." Moody's confidence in an immediate afterlife was based on the promise of Jesus and the teaching of the New Testament.

The Bible reveals that the afterlife begins immediately after life on earth ends. Jesus made this clear while He hung on the cross. One of the criminals crucified next to Him cried out, "'Jesus, remember me when you come into your kingdom.'" Jesus answered with a promise: "'Today you will be with me in paradise'" (Luke 23:42–43).

The apostle Paul echoed this promise, affirming that when Christians die they are "away from the body and at home with the Lord" (2 Corinthians 5:8).

While the soul of the believer immediately enjoys conscious and constant communion with the Lord, the Bible teaches that the resurrection of the body will not take place until Christ returns. When Jesus returns to rule the earth, each of His followers will be given a "glorious body" like Christ's resurrected body (Philippians 3:20–21).

The Bible's words on the afterlife are glorious for those who believe; however, they are grave for those who don't. Jesus told a sobering story of a man who died rich in money, but poor in faith. Instead of the joys of heaven, this man experienced the torments of hell (Luke 16:19–31). In the book of Revelation we see that all who choose to live separated from Christ on earth wind up separated from Him for all eternity (Revelation 20:11–15).

The Bible says we need not worry or wonder about where we'll spend our afterlife. John 3:16 says: "For God so loved the world that he gave his one and only Son, that whoever believes in him shall not perish but have eternal life." Those who trust in Jesus can face the afterlife with confidence, just like D.L. Moody did.

How do you explain that different faiths, including closely related faiths such as Judaism, Christianity and Islam, differ on the nature of God and what God wants from us?

Your question acknowledges a fact many people try to deny—different religions have real differences. Many contend that the various faiths are all variations on the same theme. However, even a casual examination of their core beliefs reveals that different religions diverge on the nature of God and what He wants from us.

So why the different beliefs? The Bible's answer, found in Romans 1:18–23, is that people are finite and fallen. We have a limited understanding of spiritual realities. Worse yet, we rebelled against our Creator and wound up intellectually darkened and spiritually disoriented. This disorientation shows up in our divergent religious beliefs. As fallen and finite people, we come up with ideas about God that are incomplete or incorrect.

The Bible says we'd all be hopelessly lost if left to ourselves. Thankfully, God didn't leave us to ourselves. God knew we'd never find Him, so He came looking for us. He sent us His Word through the Old Testament prophets. (Those faiths with links to the Old Testament Scriptures show some similarities in their beliefs.)

But God not only sent His written Word, He sent us Jesus, the Living Word (John 1:1). Jesus showed us what God is like since He is "the exact representation of his being" (Hebrews 1:3). Jesus also taught us what God wants; His teaching explained the Old Testament and laid the foundation for the New Testament.

Different faiths have big differences. Christians believe that faith in Jesus makes the biggest difference of all.

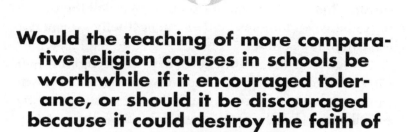

Would the teaching of more comparative religion courses in schools be worthwhile if it encouraged tolerance, or should it be discouraged because it could destroy the faith of some students?

⟩

Comparative religion courses are right to foster a relational tolerance between people of different faiths. They should encourage students to treat everyone with dignity and respect and to be kind and compassionate to others regardless of their background or beliefs. Relational tolerance is the right kind of tolerance.

Unfortunately, many comparative religion courses take tolerance too far. They do this by tolerating fuzzy thinking about different faiths. They tolerate the faulty idea that all religions are basically the same. They promote the pluralistic fantasy that different religions are just nuanced expressions of the same essence.

But as any reader of the Ask The Religion Experts column can tell, the differences between religions are substantial, not superficial. For example, only Christianity believes God became human in order to die for the sins of a broken world. To downplay the differences between faiths is neither intellectually honest nor educationally sound.

Describing the distinctions between religions will force students to evaluate their own beliefs. They will be faced with the truth that all religions cannot be equally true. While people certainly have the right to choose what they believe, it does not follow that whatever they choose to believe is right.

So what can schools do? They can offer classes that truthfully present the teachings of various religions. They can also promote kindness and compassion between people of different faiths. Finally, they must leave the choice of what to believe up to the students.

What is your faith's perspective on cremation and the burial of spouses in the same grave?

As long as funerals are a reality, funeral arrangements will be a necessity. Death forces us to make decisions.

The Bible gives us glimpses of funeral practices in the Old and New Testaments. Abraham and Sarah were buried in the same cave. Joseph was embalmed. Saul was burned. Jesus was wrapped in grave clothes and placed in a man-made cave.

While the Bible describes funerals being done, it doesn't prescribe how they must be done. While burial of the body is the norm, cremation is neither explicitly condoned or condemned. Therefore, Christians have freedom to choose the funeral arrangements that best fit their needs and desires.

While funerals cause us sorrow, Christians can face death with a living hope. Because Jesus defeated death, we will, too. Jesus said, "'I am the resurrection and the life. He who believes in me will live, even though he dies'" (John 11:25).

Because Jesus rose bodily from the grave, Christians are promised resurrected bodies. When Jesus returns, He will "transform our lowly bodies so that they will be like his glorious body" (Philippians 3:21). These new bodies will never be subject to sin, disease or death.

While we should make final arrangements for our earthly bodies, the Bible says it's more important we make future arrangements for a resurrected body by putting our trust in the risen Christ.

In your religion is faith in God enough, or is it also necessary to perform good works and love others?

A Roman prison guard once asked the apostle Paul a similar question: "'What must I do to be saved?'" Paul's answer was amazingly succinct: "'Believe in the Lord Jesus, and you will be saved'" (Acts 16:30–31).

In other words, faith in Christ is all that God requires for salvation.

That's incredibly good news. After all, most religions teach we must do certain things (rules or rituals) if we want to get things right with God.

The Christian faith says salvation comes, not because of what we do for God, but because of what Christ has done for us.

Christ's death and resurrection made salvation available for all. All we must do is respond with genuine faith in Jesus. As Paul writes in Ephesians 2:8–9:

"For it is by grace you have been saved, through faith—and this is not from yourselves, it is the gift of God—not by works, so that no one can boast."

Since salvation comes by grace through faith, does that mean love and good deeds don't matter? Not at all. While the Bible teaches that we are not saved *by* good works, it still insists that we are saved *for* good works. Ephesians 2:10 says, "For we are God's workmanship, created in Christ Jesus to do good works, which God prepared in advance for us to do."

When we genuinely trust in Christ, He transforms our lives, and the change shows up in our attitudes and actions. Faith alone saves, but the faith that saves is never alone. Saving faith is followed by a life of love and good deeds.

How are leaders selected in your faith group? How do these practices reflect its teaching?

The Bible doesn't mandate a specific selection process for church leaders. In fact, we see some variety in how leaders were chosen in the earliest churches. Sometimes apostles appointed leaders (Acts 14:23), sometimes people in the congregation helped with the selection (Acts 6:3).

The emphasis in Scripture is not on how leaders are selected but on who should be selected to lead. Here are four qualities the Bible says people need before they're ready to lead.

First, leaders need to be followers. When Jesus selected His apostles He said, "Follow Me" (Matthew 4:19; 9:9). Following Jesus means trusting Him to save and direct your life.

Second, leaders need to be servants. Jesus defined leadership as service when He said, "Whoever wants to become great among you must be your servant, and whoever wants to be first must be slave of all" (Mark 10:43–44).

Third, leaders need to have credibility. The Bible puts a leader's character ahead of his capabilities. When Paul listed requirements for leadership in 1 Timothy 3:1–13, he stressed character qualities like self-control, gentleness and faithfulness. Character is essential because Christian leadership is leadership by example (1 Peter 5:3).

Finally, leaders need to be gifted. The Bible lists "leadership" as one of the spiritual gifts God gives to some Christians to enable them to serve the church (Romans 12:8). People who follow Jesus with a servant's heart, a sterling character and a spiritual gift of leadership are the kind of Christians we want to select to lead Christ's church.

Does your faith tradition teach that men and women are equal before God, and how is that reflected in the structure and practices of your community?

The Bible teaches that men and women are equal in God's sight. Both women and men were created in God's image. Genesis 1:27 says, "So God created man in his own image, in the image of God he created him; male and female he created them." The New Testament affirms that men and women are equally heirs of the gift of life (1 Peter 3:7; Galatians 3:28).

Sadly, in our fallen world, women have often been dominated or demeaned by men. That's why Jesus' treatment of women surprised the men of His day. Instead of treating women as inferior, Jesus responded to them with compassion and respect. Jesus set an example for His church to follow. It's not surprising that where Christianity has spread, the value of women has consistently been elevated.

While God created men and women to be equal, He did not design us to be identical. He made men and women to be complementary to one another (Genesis 2:18). Our worth is the same, but our work is somewhat different in the home and the church.

In our church, we follow the instructions given in 1 Timothy 3:1–7 and appoint godly men to be pastors and elders. Women provide leadership in a wide range of teaching and caring ministries. We seek to be partners in serving Christ. Our desire is to see each man and woman enter a personal relationship with God, through Jesus, and develop healthy, productive relationships with one another in the church.

Some faiths encompass elements of divination and magic. What does your faith group believe about these issues?

The Bible forbids dabbling in divination or messing around with magic. The Old Testament is unambiguous: "Let no one be found among you who...practices divination or sorcery, interprets omens, engages in witchcraft, or casts spells, or who is a medium or spiritist or who consults the dead. Anyone who does these things is detestable to the LORD" (Deuteronomy 18:10–12). The New Testament says those who practice magic are playing with hellfire (Revelation 21:8). By the way, when the Bible condemns magic, it's referring to supernatural magic (charms, spells, sorcery) not theatrical magic (illusions, sleight of hand tricks).

So why is the Bible so down on divination and magic? Why such a strong denunciation? Here are two primary reasons. First, divination and magic attempt to do what's divine. Divination tries to discover the future, and magic attempts to control the future by occultic means. However, knowing and controlling the future are God's job. He has already given us a preview of some coming events in the book of Revelation. Now He calls us to trust Him for the part of the future that's beyond our understanding and control.

Second, divination and magic are deceptive and destructive. They open a person up to dark influences. Our culture may see Ouija boards and horoscopes as harmless, but they can be doorways to the demonic. Since the demonic is always destructive, the Bible encourages us to steer clear of divination and stay close to Jesus.

What is the difference between superstition and faith?

Some people think faith and superstition are next-door neighbours. After all, they both involve belief. But upon closer inspection, superstition and faith are miles apart. Here are three significant differences between superstition and the Christian faith.

First, superstition believes in luck, and faith believes in God. A superstitious athlete wears his "lucky" socks, believing this will bring him good luck. A Christian doesn't focus on lucky socks, but on a loving God. While luck is only an impersonal force, a Christian knows God as a personal friend.

Second, superstition offers people a way to expand their control over the future. ("Wear the socks; win the game.") Faith gives people a way to express their confidence in the God who controls the future. ("Trust

God for strength to play the game well, regardless of who wins.")

Finally, superstition is based on hunches and fantasies; faith is built on history and facts. A superstitious person can't give you the reason why a rabbit's foot is lucky or why walking under a ladder is unlucky. Christians can give you reasons for their faith. Reasons rooted in the historical events of Jesus' life—His birth, miracles, death and resurrection.

While faith is more than reason, there are reasons for a Christian's faith. Faith sure beats knocking on wood.

How do we know whether God has answered our prayers?

A recent edition of *Time* magazine had a cover story titled "A Nation Of Prayer."[1] The article reported that sixty-six percent of Canadians pray. How can those who pray know whether God has answered their prayers?

Let's say you ask God to heal a friend who's undergoing treatments for cancer. If he or she recovers, was it God or the chemo that made the difference?

The Bible says, "Every good and perfect gift is from above, coming down from the Father of the heavenly lights" (James 1:17). So the good gift of healing is from God, though He may have used doctors and medicines in the process. Physicians can treat illness, but only God can heal it (Psalm 103:3).

---

[1] *Time*, "A Nation of Prayer," November 24, 2003.

But what if healing doesn't come? Does that mean God hasn't answered? Not at all. The Bible tells us of a time when the apostle Paul earnestly asked God to remove a thorny problem from his life. God answered his prayer, but not how Paul expected. God said "no" to removing the problem. But He said "yes" to strengthening Paul in the midst of his troubles (2 Corinthians 12:7–10).

The Bible tells us that there's one prayer that God always answers with a resounding "yes." Romans 10:9,13 says, "If you confess with your mouth, 'Jesus is Lord,' and believe in your heart that God raised him from the dead, you will be saved…. Everyone who calls on the name of the Lord will be saved."

A sincere prayer for salvation is one God always answers.

What is your faith's perspective on organ donation? Would you encourage your members to consider it for humanity's sake?

When the Bible was written, organ donation wasn't a medical possibility. Had it been, there were Christians who would have donated their eyes to the apostle Paul. In Galatians 4:15, Paul writes, "I can testify that, if you could have done so, you would have torn out your eyes and given them to me."

Organ donation is one way Christians can live out the command to love others. In 1 John 3:16 we are told, "This is how we know what love is: Jesus Christ laid down his life for us. And we ought to lay down our lives for our brothers." Laying down our lives involves sacrifice and generosity. Organ donation is one way to give of ourselves to help others.

The reason Christians are told to lay down their lives for others is because Jesus laid down His life for us. In the greatest "donation" ever, Jesus gave His body and blood for us. The night before He was crucified, He said, "'This is my body given for you'" (Luke 22:19). His death made eternal life possible for all who believe in Him. "For God so loved the world that he gave his one and only Son, that whoever believes in him shall not perish but have eternal life" (John 3:16).

Those of us who have received life through Christ's death have good reason to be good donors. We should give our hearts to love people while we live and give our organs to help them when we die.

If one has sinned, how does one reconcile with God?

I know this will sound grim, but you can't. Once you've sinned, you can't reconcile yourself to God. That means all of us are in big trouble, because all of us have sinned. "For all have sinned and fall short of the glory of God" (Romans 3:23). You may be a good person, but you're not sinless. And that's a serious problem because "the wages of sin is death" (Romans 6:23).

When people start feeling the guilt of their sin, they often turn to religion. Since most religions have laws and rules, many people think they can reconcile themselves to God by keeping those laws. But it won't work.

Our best attempts at keeping religious laws aren't good enough for God. The Bible is blunt when it says, "Clearly no one is justified before God by the law" (Galatians 3:11).

But don't give up. There is good news. God has done for us what we could not do for ourselves. He made reconciliation possible by sending Jesus to pay for our sins. 2 Corinthians 5:19 says, "God was reconciling the world to himself in Christ, not counting men's sins against them." Because of Jesus' death on our behalf, God offers us complete forgiveness and close friendship.

Reconciliation with God is not achieved by works; it's accepted by faith. When we trust in Jesus, we are reconciled to God and can echo the words of Romans 5:11: "We also rejoice in God through our Lord Jesus Christ, through whom we have now received reconciliation."

What does your faith teach about revenge and forgiveness?

Revenge seems quite natural to us. Someone causes us pain and we start thinking about payback. Insult for insult. Violence for violence. The result is our broken and bloodstained world.

Jesus taught us to reject revenge. He called us to love our enemies, to pray for those who make our lives miserable (Matthew 5:44). Jesus' words about forgiveness seem counterintuitive. Some would say they're counterproductive. Why should we opt for forgiveness rather than revenge? Here are three good reasons.

First, God will take care of payback. Romans 12:19 says, "Do not take revenge, my friends, but leave room for God's wrath, for it is written: 'It is mine to avenge; I will repay.' says the Lord." God has authorized government to punish evildoers (Romans 13:4). Even when government gets it wrong, God will get it right. There is a judgment day coming (Hebrews 9:27).

Second, forgiveness sets us free. Revenge locks up our souls in bitterness and malice. Forgiveness unlocks the door. For a graphic case study of this, read Matthew 18:21–35.

Finally, we forgive because we've been forgiven. Jesus offered us forgiveness when He could have sought revenge. He was brutalized and crucified, and yet He still cried, "Father, forgive them" (Luke 23:34). By believing in Christ, we can receive God's forgiveness. Once we've experienced forgiveness, we are to extend it to others. Ephesians 4:32 says, "Be kind and compassionate to one another, forgiving each other, just as in Christ God forgave you."

Revenge is natural. Forgiveness is supernatural.

Same-sex marriages have been approved by courts in British Columbia, Ontario and Quebec. Should the clergy of your faith perform same-sex marriages to stay in tune with the times?

Modifying marriage to stay in tune with the times is not really a new idea. In Jesus' day, some religious leaders argued that the historical understanding of marriage was too restrictive.

When asked for His view, Jesus responded,

"Haven't you read...that at the beginning the Creator 'made them male and female,' and said, 'For this reason a man will leave his father and mother and be united to his wife, and the two will become one flesh'? So they are no longer two, but one. Therefore what God has joined together, let man not separate" (Matthew 19:4–6).

Jesus' words point us back to God's original intent for marriage. He reminds us that marriage was God's idea. As the designer of marriage, God has the right to be the definer of marriage. And He has defined marriage as the permanent union of a man and a woman. Redefining marriage to include same-sex unions would violate God's enduring vision for marriage.

But don't the clergy need to stay in tune with the changing times? While members of the clergy need to be in touch with the times, they cannot always be in tune with them. They should stay in touch with the needs and challenges people face today. But they must stay in tune with what is timeless.

Musicians tell us that musical tones are fixed at certain frequencies. For example the tone "A" is always 440 hertz. Unless instruments are tuned to this fixed reference point, they will only produce a dissonant cacophony of sounds.

If we hope to help marriages make beautiful music, then we will need to help them stay in tune, not with the ever-changing times, but with God's timeless truth.

Several evangelical Christian groups have gone to Iraq to help rebuild that country after the war. Are these groups taking advantage of the collapse of the Iraqi government to spread their faith? If so, should that be allowed?

Christian compassion is nothing new. It can be traced back to Christ Himself. When Jesus walked our earth, He modeled a life of compassionate service; He healed many who were sick or suffering. Jesus also called His followers to live lives marked by love. He made it clear that the greatest commandment was to love God above all else and to love your neighbour as yourself (Mark 12:30–31).

Following the example of Christ, Christians have consistently given compassionate service to people in need. Where suffering has been most acute, Christians have been most active: supplying relief aid or helping relieve the suffering of AIDS, treating leprosy or teaching literacy, providing clean water for the thirsty or food for the hungry.

If evangelical Christians are involved in helping rebuild the lives of people in Iraq, they would simply be doing what followers of Christ have done for centuries.

Though most people commend Christians for showing compassion, some are concerned they will also try to spread their faith. Some would say to Christians, "Bring your food, but not your faith." This kind of thinking draws a false dichotomy between physical and spiritual needs. It fails to treat people in a holistic matter. It misses the fact that people have hungry souls, not just hungry stomachs.

Jesus spoke of this spiritual hunger when He said, "'I am the bread of life. He who comes to me will never go hungry, and he who believes in me will never be thirsty'" (John 6:35).

Because of God's love, evangelical Christians are eager to help those who are physically hungry. However, that same love causes us to be sensitive to those who are spiritually hungry. To do less would be less than loving.

We often hear the term "final judgment." How does your faith group view God as a judge over mankind?

The Bible pictures final judgment as a future reality and a frightening prospect. After death, we're scheduled for a day in God's court. "Man is destined to die once, and after that to face judgment" (Hebrews 9:27). The apostle John saw a vision of what judgment day will be like. "Then I saw a great white throne and him who was seated on it.... I saw the dead, great and small, standing before the throne, and books were opened" (Revelation 20:11–12).

Final judgment will be painfully thorough. Our actions will be assessed: "God 'will give to each person according to what he has done'" (Romans 2:6). Our secrets will be revealed: "God will judge men's secrets" (Romans 2:16). Our every word will be weighed: "'But I tell you that men will have to give account on the day of judgment for every careless word'" (Matthew 12:36).

Since God's judgment will be thorough, we're all in big trouble. We've all sinned (Romans 3:23). And the penalty for sinning against God is eternal separation from Him in hell (Matthew 18:8).

But don't despair. There's hope. Jesus said there's a way to be safe on judgment day. "'Truly, truly, I say to you, he who hears My word, and believes Him who sent Me, has eternal life, and does not come into judgment, but has passed out of death into life'" (John 5:24 NAS).

Those who trust in Jesus now, will not face God's judgment in the future.

How can you call God a loving God when He knows the pain and suffering to be created by the hurricanes, floods and diseases that He either creates or allows?

Our world has certainly been deluged with disasters lately: hurricanes, floods, earthquakes and volcanic activity. Are these disasters really "acts of God" and if so, why wouldn't He take action to stop them?

The Bible says our earth is going through labour pains. "We know that the whole creation has been groaning as in the pains of childbirth right up to the present time" (Romans 8:22). Disasters indicate creation is having contractions.

What's the reason for these catastrophic contractions? The Bible traces the problem to human sin. When our first parents disobeyed God (Genesis 3:19), they brought death to the world and pain to the planet. Sin put the earth out of sync (Romans 8:20).

If God is loving, why doesn't He stop creation's contractions? He allows disaster, and even sends it (see Isaiah 45:7), to show us how vulnerable we are. He loves us enough to dispel our illusion that we can live without Him. C.S. Lewis once wrote, "God whispers to us in our pleasures, speaks in our conscience, but shouts in our pains: it is his megaphone to rouse a deaf world."[1] Natural disasters warn us to get right with God and avoid eternal disaster.

The Bible assures us that earth's labour pains won't last forever. God promises to recreate the heavens and earth and remove all sin and suffering (Isaiah 65:17; Revelation 21:1–4).

Those who genuinely trust in God's Son, Jesus, are given a home in the new creation, a place where disaster will never strike again.

---

[1] C.S. Lewis, *The Problem Of Pain*.

Do all sins have equal weight, or does your faith group categorize sins?

Categorizing sin is a bit like categorizing cancer. No matter how you label them, they're all bad. While some sins seem less deadly than others, all are destructive.

Some sins are slower to show their damaging effects, but all cause spiritual sickness. If untreated, all sin leads to death. The Bible makes that clear when it warns, "sin, when it is full-grown, gives birth to death" (James 1:15).

Since all sin is deadly, we can't just speak of "seven deadly sins." If we try to develop a "sindex" that ranks various sins, we may miss the point that every sin is spiritually malignant.

We may also dodge the diagnosis that God makes about our lives—all of us are terminally ill because of sin. "For all have sinned and fall short of the glory of God" (Romans 3:23).

While there may be different cures for cancer, there is only one cure for sin. Jesus' death on the cross provides the spiritual remedy we all need (Hebrews 9:28). He offers spiritual healing and eternal life to all who choose to become His followers by faith.

While all sins are serious, rejecting Jesus as God's Son and Saviour is the worst sin of all. This is the one sin for which there is no cure. It's an "eternal sin" that will never be forgiven (Mark 3:29).

Thankfully, no one needs to commit this unpardonable sin. Instead, we can all have our sins pardoned by trusting Jesus as the healer of our souls.

Faith groups differ on whether there are many gods, one God, a God who is three-in-one or an unknowable god. Why are there such differences?

The opening verse in the Bible declares, "In the beginning God created the heavens and the earth" (Genesis 1:1). God also created people, giving us the ability to relate to Him in a personal way. Tragically, the first humans misunderstood and misused freedom. They sinned against Him and stumbled into darkness.

Over time, the human understanding of God became clouded and confused. Romans 1:21–23 gives this indictment:

> For although they knew God, they neither glorified Him as God nor gave thanks to Him, but their thinking became futile and their foolish hearts were darkened. Although they claimed to be wise, they became fools and exchanged the glory of the immortal God for images made

to look like mortal man and birds and animals and reptiles.

Monotheism gave way to polytheism.

In *The Origin and Growth of Religion*, anthropologist Wilhelm Schmidt documents how numerous cultures, which now worship many gods, originally worshipped one creator God.[1] The *Encyclopedia of Religion and Ethics* reports that in ancient Chinese culture people worshipped Shang Ti, whom they understood to be the creator and lawgiver.[2] Even in Incan culture, monotheism predated polytheism.

Thankfully, God did not want to be an unknowable God. He sent His Son, Jesus, and His Holy Spirit to reveal His nature (three-in-one) and draw us back to a personal relationship with Him.

[1] Wilhelm Schmidt, *The Origin And Growth Of Religion: Facts And Theories*.

[2] *The Encyclopedia Of Religions And Ethics*.

Much has been said of late about the Charter of Rights and Freedoms. What does your faith group teach about individual and collective rights?

The basis for individual and collective rights is found in a document much older than the Charter of Rights and Freedom. The Bible speaks about individual and collective rights. It explains that these rights are bestowed by our Creator, not simply granted by the state.

Because "the LORD is a God of justice" (Isaiah 30:18), He requires that humans treat one another with justice. "He has showed you, O man, what is good. And what does the LORD require of you? To act justly and to love mercy and to walk humbly with your God" (Micah 6:8).

However, instead of demanding our own rights, the Bible calls us to defend the rights of others. Christians are called to stand up for the rights of those who are most vulnerable: the widow, the orphan, the alien, the unborn and the poor. "The righteous care about justice for the poor" (Proverbs 29:7)

Since our human rights are linked to our Creator, they are limited by Him as well. We don't have the right to do what God says is wrong. That's why we must respect the spiritual, social and sexual limits He establishes for us. His will is higher than our wants.

There is one right that God says we all have. That's the right to become part of His family by putting our faith in Jesus. John 1:12 says, "To those who believed in his name, he gave the right to become children of God."

It was recently reported that a devil-worshipping non-commissioned officer in the Royal Navy has become the first registered Satanist in the British armed forces. Is this taking the concept of multi-faith acceptance too far? And would you support the Canadian navy taking such an action?

Britain's navy recently sailed into spiritually uncharted waters by permitting an officer to register as a practicing Satanist. In doing so, they sanctioned a belief system that, according to the officer, involved "treachery" and "indulgence" as two of its core values. It's hard to see how these vices can be of value to a navy whose sailors must be trustworthy and self-controlled.

How could Her Majesty's Royal Navy have gotten so far off course? They adopted a policy of not only registering, but also accepting, all faiths.

Having welcomed all religions on board, they couldn't find a good reason to keep Satanism off. They got lost in a sea of religious pluralism.

Religious pluralism is a viewpoint with inherent problems. It's based on the assumption that all religious views are equally worthy. Taken to an extreme, this means worshipping the devil is as valid as worshipping Jesus.

Pluralism also requires a redefinition of the word *tolerance*. Tolerance used to mean "everyone has a right to his or her opinion." The word now means "everyone's opinion is right." Common sense says this new definition won't float.

Canada is already sailing under the flag of religious pluralism. If we want to avoid a spiritual shipwreck, we'd be wise to alter our course. We can have our military focus on evaluating behaviour rather than belief systems. We can treat everyone as equally valuable, without affirming every belief system as equally valid. We can pray that God guides all who seek Him towards the Truth.

When is anger truly righteous and acceptable?

Anger is righteous when it is an echo of God's righteous anger. The Bible tells us that while God is slow to anger (Psalm 103:8), He is angered by wickedness (Psalm 106:29). Jesus was angry with those who distorted the truth and discarded human needs (Mark 3:5). Since humans were created in God's image, we have a capacity for righteous anger.

The problem is that most of the time our anger isn't all that righteous. James 1:20 warns that "man's anger does not bring about the righteous life that God desires."

Often our anger is tainted and toxic. Our anger is like a strong chemical that is both explosive and corrosive. When we get angry, our relationships can be blown up. And our souls can get eaten away.

So how do we make sure our anger is appropriate? How do we keep it from being contaminated by selfishness or sinfulness? We begin by bringing our anger to God. Psalm 62:8 tells us to pour out our hearts to the Lord. As we pour out our hearts to God, He can start to neutralize the acidic aspects of our anger that make it so explosive or corrosive. Jesus can clean up the toxins in our anger, so that we act in a way that is constructive rather than destructive.

Strong chemicals come with a warning label that reads, "handle with care." Anger comes with a warning label as well: "handle with prayer."

How can we find spiritual peace?

Your question resonates deeply inside many hearts. We all long for a spiritual peace that stabilizes and strengthens our lives. The good news is that God wants to give us the peace we need. On the first Christmas night, God sent angels to proclaim a message of peace on earth (Luke 2:14). He also gave us the gift of Jesus— the one the prophet Isaiah called the "Prince of Peace" (Isaiah 9:6). Jesus brings the peace we need: "'Peace I leave with you; my peace I give you'" (John 14:27).

But in order to receive peace from God, you must first make peace with God. The Bible makes it painfully clear that all of us have sinned (Romans 3:23). Our sins have separated us from God and His gift of peace. "'There is no peace,' says the LORD 'for the wicked'" (Isaiah 48:22).

How do you make peace with God? You turn from your sin and turn to the Lord Jesus in simple, sincere faith. Romans 5:1 says, "Therefore, since we have been justified through faith, we have peace with God through our Lord Jesus Christ."

Once you've made peace with God through faith in Jesus, you can continually pray and ask Him to fill your heart with His peace.

> Do not be anxious about anything, but in everything, by prayer and petition, with thanksgiving, present your requests to God. And the peace of God, which transcends all understanding, will guard your hearts and your minds in Christ Jesus (Philippians 4:6–7).

Should we bring faith into the workplace? If so, how should it be done?

Bringing faith into the workplace is good for business. According to research done by Merrill Oster, a former *Inc. Magazine* Entrepreneur Of The Year, executives who intentionally applied religious teachings at work scored higher on almost all leadership measurement instruments. Leaders who took their faith to work also ranked higher in personal job satisfaction and net worth. Bringing faith to work pays off.

But just how should faith be brought into the workplace? Let me highlight three ways Christians are to take their faith to work.

First, Christians are to be industrious on the job. The Bible instructs Christians to work hard. "Whatever you do, work at it with all your heart, as working for the Lord, not for men" (Colossians 3:23).

Second, Christians are to have integrity as they work. Jesus wants His followers to be exemplary in their ethics (1 Peter 2:11–12). I know a Christian man who refused to lie for his boss. When his boss got irate, he said, "Look, I won't lie for you, but I won't lie to you, either." His faith bolstered his honesty.

Finally, Christians are to be interested in others at work. Employees often carry heavy concerns with them when they show up at the office. At appropriate times— during a break or over lunch—Christians can offer them the encouragement and hope that springs from their faith in Jesus.

Trying to keep faith out of the workplace is simply bad business. Companies and co-workers benefit when faith goes to work.

Why is the world so lacking in love?

I grew up hearing Diana Ross sing, "What the world needs now is love, sweet love. It's the only thing that there's just too little of." If we had a shortage of love thirty years ago, we're in even more desperate need of it today.

The kind of love our broken world needs is not merely sentimental or superficial. We need a love that is sacrificial. We need a love that isn't just reserved for those who like us (or who are just like us). We need a love that doesn't wither when relationships heat up. We need a love that is strong enough to absorb pain and not retaliate.

This kind of love doesn't come naturally to us. It only comes supernaturally. It comes from God, because God is love (1 John 4:7–8).

God demonstrated what true love looks like when He sent us His Son, Jesus. "This is love: not that we loved God, but that he loved us and sent his Son as an atoning sacrifice for our sins" (1 John 4:10).

When we respond to God's love by trusting in Christ Jesus, He promises to pour out His love into our hearts by the Holy Spirit (Romans 5:5). He fills and refills us with the love we need. His love gives us both a reason and the resources to love others. As 1 John 4:19 says, "We love because he first loved us."

When God's love fills people's hearts, it will make a world of difference.

Here's a few Good Questions for You!

In this book, you've had the chance to read my answers to a number of spiritual questions. I'd like to wrap things up by asking *you* a few good questions.

Do you desire to have a personal, life-changing relationship with God?

If you do, you're not alone. Many of us have a deep longing for a relationship with God. I'm convinced that God stirs a longing for Himself inside of us. He wants us to want Him. Augustine, one of the early Christian leaders, put it well when he said that God made us for Himself and our hearts are restless until they find rest in Him.

Do you realize you don't deserve to be close to God?

If your heart is sensitive and sincere, you're aware that you haven't always lived up to your own ideals, let alone to God's standards. God is perfect and so He's worthy of perfection. But perfection is beyond us. We've all messed up in large and small ways. The Bible labels our shortcomings as "sin." And it's quite clear that "all have sinned and fall short of the glory of God" (Romans 3:23). That means that all of us are in trouble with God. None of us deserve to be close to Him.

Do you understand that Jesus is your only hope for getting things right with God?

Jesus made a claim that, on the surface, seems outlandishly exclusive. He said, "I am the way and the truth and the life. No one comes to the Father but through me" (John 14:6). Jesus said He is our only hope for getting close to God. That's an amazing statement. But then again, Jesus is amazing. He lived a perfect life and then died a perfectly horrific death. He willingly chose to die, saying His death would pay for the sins of the whole world (Mark 10:35; 1 John 2:2). Jesus' resurrection gives credibility to His claims. It gives us good reason to believe He is the way to get close to God.

Are you ready to admit your need and trust in Jesus?

You can enter a life-changing relationship with God today by confessing your sin and trusting in Jesus as your only hope for a rela-